A taste of DEV

C000001563

Recipes

River Teign Mussels with a Saffron, Cream & Cider Sauce	*pp 7*
Potted Devon Crab	*pp 9*
Devon Crab Cakes with Crème Fraiche & Chive Dressing	*pp 10*
Brown Crab, Samphire & Asparagus Salad	*pp 12*
Seared Scallops with Black Pudding & Celariac	*pp 13*
Lobster Thermidor	*pp 16*
Mediterranean Style Fish Soup	*pp 18*
Tandoori Spiced Salmon	*pp 21*
Fishermans Pie	*pp 27*
Dartmouth Pie	*pp 29*
Exeter Stew with Herby Doughboys	*pp 30*
Thyme Roasted Loin of Pork with Devon Cider	*pp 32*
Devon Laver Cakes	*pp 33*
Devonshire Cream Tea	*pp 33*
Strawberry Jam	*pp 35*
Whitepot (Baked Rice Pudding)	*pp 36*

Recipes

Newton Abbot Cider Cake   *pp 38*
Raspberry Ripple & Clotted Cream Ice Cream   *pp 39*
Devonshire Splits   *pp 40*
Devonish Junket/Damask Cream   *pp 41*
Devonish Clotted Cream Fudge   *pp 42*
Barnstaple Fair Pears   *pp 44*
Exeter Pudding   *pp 46*

Text by Stuart Adlington. First published in 2011.
This edition published in 2011 by Myriad Books.
© Myriad Books Ltd 2011
PRINTED IN CHINA

Publishers Disclaimer
Whilst every effort has been made to ensure that the information contained is correct, the publisher cannot be held responsible for any errors and or omissions. Please note certain recipes may contain nuts or nut oil. The photographs in this book are for illustrative purposes only and do not represent the finished recipe. Photographs © Getty Images and Shutterstock.

A taste of....

One of England's largest counties, and undoubtedly one of England's most picturesque, Devon, situated between Cornwall to the West and Somerset and Dorset to the East has many foods and dishes in common with it's close neighbours, however Devon without doubt has a strong heritage and culinary history maintaining a fiercely independent attitude in preserving its local dishes and culinary heritage.

Clotted cream is probably the most synonymous of all the foods associated with the County of Devon, rich, creamy and totally indulgent, thickly spread on warm scones served with home-made strawberry jam is surely one of life's great pleasures.

A visit to Devon would surely not be complete with savouring a Devonshire cream tea. Devon is also famous for the beautiful little yeast risen buns filed with cream and jam called Devonshire Splits. Regional specialities also include Barnstaple Fair Pears, gently simmered in red wine or cider and Damask Cream, a subtle dessert flavoured with rose water.

It is no surprise that with an abundance of rich dairy milk, the region also produces some of the finest cheeses to be found anywhere in the land.

Devon is also renowned for it's traditional production of Scrumpy and Cider originally made using windfall apples found in the abundant orchards scattered around the County. Another famous beverage from the region is Plymouth Gin, the traditional drink of the Royal Navy. After 200 years the Gin is still produced in the oldest Gin distillery operating in the world.

The beautiful coastline of both North and South Devon is home to many picturesque fishing villages and coastal resorts. With such a wealth of fresh seafood literally on its doorstep it is no wonder that fish is a major part of the local diet with a rich and diverse selection of the freshest possible seafood available all year round.

Long gone are the days when rich shoals of mackerel and herring provided the region with fame and fortune, however small fishing boats still operate bringing in the daily catch of the day.

Devon also boasts the beautiful yet rugged diverse landscapes of both Exmoor and Dartmoor providing a wealth of delicious game birds and the rich Devon pasture land are home to the prized Devon Red Cattle providing some of the finest beef in the land. Devon without doubt has a rich and diverse cultural history and heritage, fiercely proud of their local produce and without question a place of inspiration for food lovers everywhere.

RIVER TEIGN MUSSELS WITH A SAFFRON, CREAM AND CIDER SAUCE

Serves 4

Such a simple, but delicious lunch or supper dish. Soft plump, juicy River Teign mussels cooked in a cream sauce flavoured with saffron and cider. Serve with crusty bread to mop up all the lovely juices.

Ingredients
2kg/4lb 4oz mussels, cleaned, de-bearded, discard any that don't close when tapped
4 shallots, peeled, finely chopped
2 garlic cloves, peeled, crushed
200ml/7fl oz cider
a good pinch of fresh saffron
50g/2oz butter
5fl oz/1/4 pint fresh double cream
5fl oz/1/4 pint fish stock
fresh chopped parsley

1. In a large pan, melt the butter, add the chopped shallots and garlic and fry gently for 2-3 minutes until tender but not coloured. Add the saffron, fish stock and cider and bring to the boil.

2. Reduce the mixture by half, then add the cream and return to the boil. Add the mussels to the pan and place a tight fitting lid on the pan, then give the pan a really good shake.

3. Cook the mussels for 3-4 minutes or until they have opened , Remove the mussels with a slotted spoon and set aside. Discard any mussels that have not opened.

4. Gently heat the sauce until it has reduced and thickened slightly, season to taste with salt if required and plenty of freshly ground black pepper.

5. Place the mussels into a large warmed serving bowl and pour the cream sauce over the top. Sprinkle with freshly chopped parsley and serve immediately with fresh crusty bread.

POTTED DEVON CRAB
Serves 4

A deliciously simple dish packed full of flavour, spiced crabmeat simply eaten with hot toast, the perfect light lunch or supper dish.

Ingredients
400g/14oz crabmeat
200g/7oz butter, melted
good pinch of cayenne pepper
zest and juice of half a lemon
pinch of salt
pinch of mace
pinch of nutmeg
extra melted butter to finish

1. Melt the butter, add the cayenne pepper, mace, nutmeg and lemon zest, mix well and set aside.

2. Add the lemon juice to the crabmeat and season with salt and freshly ground black pepper. Fold in the melted butter into the crabmeat and spoon into individual ramekins, refrigerate until set.

3. Seal each dish by pouring over a little clarified butter, then refrigerate again for an hour or two until ready to serve. Simply serve with hot toast.

DEVON CRAB CAKES WITH A CRÈME FRAICHE AND CHIVE DRESSING

Serves 4

Deliciously simple crab cakes served with a light refreshing crème fraiche dressing flavoured with chives. A wonderful light lunch or supper dish.

Ingredients
350g/12oz crab meat
110g/4oz mashed potato, cooled
2 tbsps fresh chopped coriander
pinch of cayenne pepper
flour to dredge
1 egg beaten
sunflower oil for frying

For the dressing
110ml crème fraiche
1 tbsp lemon juice
2 tbsps chopped fresh chives
lemon or lime wedges to serve

1. In a large bowl combine the cooled mashed potato with the crab meat, cayenne pepper and coriander and stir in the beaten egg.

2. Do not overwork the mixture as you want the crab meat to retain a little texture. Season with salt and freshly ground black pepper.

3. Dust the mixture with a little flour and form into 4 patties. Heat a small amount of oil in a frying pan and fry the crab cakes over a medium heat for 2-3 minutes on either side until lightly golden brown.

4. Meanwhile combine the crème fraiche with the lemon juice and stir in the chopped fresh chives. Remove the crab cakes from the frying pan and drain on absorbent kitchen paper to remove any excess oil.

5. Serve with cakes with a generous spoonful of the dressing on the side and a wedge of lemon.

BROWN CRAB, ASPARAGUS AND SAMPHIRE SALAD
Serves 4

Ingredients
1 x large brown cooked crab, meat removed
350g/12oz fresh asparagus
225g/8oz samphire ,picked and washed
1 garlic clove, peeled and crushed
2 tbsps olive oil
juice of half a lemon
parmesan shavings to garnish
chopped fresh parsley

1. Remove the hard woody ends from the asparagus, the easiest way to do this is to snap them off with your fingers, the asparagus will break where the woody end joins the tender stalk.

2. Bring a large pan of boiling salted water to the boil and cook the asparagus and samphire for one minutes. Drain well and refresh under cold running water this will help retain the beautiful green colour and prevent them from cooking further.

3. Place the drained asparagus and samphire in a large bowl and dress with the olive oil and lemon juice. Season with flaked sea salt and a generous twist of freshly ground black pepper.

4. To serve, divide the asparagus and samphire between 4 serving plates, then arrange the white and dark crab meat over the top. Sprinkle over the chopped fresh parsley, drizzle over a little extra olive oil and scatter with the shaved parmesan shavings.

SEARED SCALLOPS, BLACK PUDDING WITH CELARIAC AND APPLE PURÉE

Serves 4

A wonderful combination, makes the most wonderful starter and so simple to prepare but looks so impressive and tastes delicious. It is very important not to overcook the scallops though.

Ingredients
12 fresh scallops, cleaned
8 small slices of black pudding, the same size of the scallops
olive oil
salt and pepper
knob of butter
small handful fresh pea shoots to garnish

For the purée
150g/5oz celariac, peeled and diced
200ml chicken stock
1 tsp curry powder
20g/2oz butter
225g/8oz bramley apples, peeled, cored and sliced
splash of double cream

1. To make the purée, place the celariac in a saucepan with the chicken stock and curry powder, simmer for about

20 minutes or until tender then drain well.

2. Meanwhile fry the sliced apples in the butter for 5 minutes until soft, then transfer the apples and celariac to a food processor, add a small splash of cream, then blend until smooth. Season with salt and freshly ground pepper to taste. Set aside and keep warm.

3. Heat a large frying pan, add a knob of butter, then fry the slices of black pudding for 2-3 minutes until lightly crisp on both sides, remove from the pan and transfer to a plate lined with kitchen paper. Season the scallops with salt and pepper, then rub with the olive oil.

4. Wipe out the pan used to cook the black pudding, then heat until smoking hot, add a small knob of butter to the pan, then sear the scallops for 1 minute on either side until lightly golden brown and caramelised. Remove from the pan and place on the paper with the black pudding.

5. To serve, place a spoonful of the celariac purée in the centre of a warmed plate, neatly arrange 2 slices of the black pudding and 3 scallops on top of the purée.

6. Gently place a small bunch of the pea shoots on top of the dish and drizzle a little olive oil over the top. Serve immediately.

LOBSTER

Lobster, undoubtedly the king of all crustaceans and this dish is a true classic, once eaten never forgotten. If you can use source a live lobster and are willing to pay the price, and not too frightened to kill the poor thing, then I suggest you do. There are a few simple cooking rules which must be applied.

The official sanctioned method of killing them is to place them in the freezer for a couple of hours to reduce them to a trance like state, then place them in a pan of rapidly boiling salted water, ideally sea water but alternatively fresh water with salt added to a ratio of 30gr to 1 litre will suffice.

Cooking times vary by weight, 12 minutes for a medium sized lobster of 500g, 15 minutes for anything up to 750g, and an extra 5 minutes for 500g after that. There are many ways to enjoy lobster, some romantic, some classic and some deeply indulgent. Cold lobster with a good mayonnaise is hard to beat, but the white meat is so rich and robust will stand up to all manners of spicing and sophisticated sauces.

Many people often tend to indulge in only the white meat found in the claws and tail, however there are many other delights to be found: the creamy meat inside the head, the browny grey liver inside the body, and the pink coral that often lines the shell of the female lobster. The only bits you can't eat are the dark gut that runs along the top of the tail, (and is easily removed), the small gritty sack just behind the mouth, and the gills (similar to the dead men's fingers in a crab but smaller). As long as it is very fresh and not overcooked you can't go far wrong.

LOBSTER THERMIDOR
Serves 2

Ingredients	*For the Béchamel sauce*
1 live Lobster (1-1.5 kg)	1 onion, peeled, finely chopped
25g/1oz butter	1 celery stick finely chopped
1 small glass of white wine	1 bay leaf
1 tbsp double cream	500ml full cream milk
1 tsp English mustard	50g/2oz butter
2 shallots, finely chopped	50g/2oz plain flour
pinch of cayenne pepper	
50g/2oz grated gruyere cheese	
1 sprig of fresh tarragon, finely chopped	
salt and freshly ground black pepper	
200ml thick béchamel sauce	
(recipe below)	

1. Place the chopped onions and celery in a pan with the bay leaf and milk; bring to the boil, then take the pan off the heat and leave to infuse for about an hour, then strain the milk. Melt the butter in a separate pan and stir in the flour, cook this gently for a couple of minutes then gradually whisk in the milk a little at a time, to get a nice smooth sauce. Let it simmer for 5 minutes, if its to thick add a touch more hot milk. Season to taste with salt and freshly ground pepper and set aside.

2. Kill and cook your lobster as described previously and leave to cool (if you can't get fresh, then a pre cooked lobster will do, but will not be the same quality). Twist off the claws, crack them with a hammer or nutcrackers and remove the meat, set this aside. The body of the lobster should be split lengthways along

the lateral line with a large, heavy and very sharp knife. This is most easily done if you lay the lobster on its back on a large chopping board. Press the point of the knife into the tip of the tail, and bring the knife down the length of the lobster, dissecting it evenly between the two sets of legs, do this carefully so as not to damage the shell.

3. Once you are through the flesh to the shell at the back of the lobster press hard on the knife to cut through the shell, you may want to use a pair of kitchen scissors to snip through any bits of shell that are not quite cut through. Carefully remove the tail meat from each half of the lobster, chop roughly and add to the claw meat. Scrape any brown meat from the head along with the pink coral and add this also to the claw meat. Remove any nasty bits as mentioned above and you will be left with 2 empty shell halves, with plenty of space in the head and tail cavities to replace the finished meat.

4. In a frying pan cook the shallots in the butter over a medium heat until softened and very lightly browned, add the wine and simmer and reduce until only a tablespoon of liquid remains. Stir in 200ml of the béchamel sauce, the double cream plus the mustard and tarragon and allow to bubble in the pan for just a minute. Remove from the heat and stir in three quarters of the grated cheese and the cayenne pepper. Mix in all the meat from the lobster until it is well coated with the sauce, season to taste with salt and black pepper.

5. Divide the meat back into the 2 half shells, sprinkle with the remainder of the cheese and place under a hot grill for about 5-10 minutes, until brown and bubbling. Serve at once.

MEDITERRANEAN STYLE FISH SOUP
Serves 8-10

A wonderful fish soup using a selection of some of the finest seafood from around the coast of Devon, however this recipe can easily be adapted to suit your tastes and your budget. Admittedly there is plenty of preparation before hand and a multitude of ingredients but please trust me the end result is simply magnificent.

Ingredients
1 red mullet, filleted approx 350g/12oz in weight
1 gurnard, filleted, approx 450g/1lb
1 small monkfish tail, skin removed, approx 450g/1lb
110g/4oz prepared squid
20 mussels, cleaned, de-bearded
150ml/5fl oz white wine
2.5 ltr fish stock
1 fennel bulb, trimmed, cut into 8 wedges
1 red onion, peeled, cut into 8 wedges
1 leek, trimmed, chopped
1 celery sticks, trimmed, chopped
1 red pepper, de-seeded, chopped
5 plum tomatoes, skin removed, chopped
6 small new potatoes, cut into quarters
120ml/4fl oz olive oil
6 garlic cloves, peeled, crushed
zest of an orange
pinch of chilli flakes
2 tbsps tomato purée
2 bay leaves

sprig of fresh thyme
2 tbsps chopped fresh dill or fennel tops
3 tbsps pernod or ricard
ciabatta bread to serve

1. Begin by cutting the fish fillets and squid into bite sized pieces ensuring they are all the same size - this will ensure they all cook evenly. Place the mussels in a pan with a splash of wine, cover and cook over a high heat for 3-4 minutes or until the mussels have opened. Discard any that remain closed. Strain the mussel cooking liquor and retain, then pick the meat from the shells reserving a few left in the shells.

2. Heat the oil in a large pan, add the fennel, onions, celery, red pepper, garlic, orange zest and dried chilli flakes. Fry for 3-4 minutes or until the vegetables are just softened.

3. Add the tomato paste, fish stock, the remaining wine and liquor from the mussels, potatoes and tomatoes. Season with salt if required and lots of freshly ground black pepper. Bring to the boil and simmer for 5 minutes.

4. Add the fish, plus the bay leaves, thyme and half the chopped dill or fennel tops together with the pernod. Simmer for 3 minutes only as you don't want to overcook the fish, adding the mussels meat and the retained mussels in their shells for the last 30 seconds just to warm through.

5. Sprinkle over the remaining chopped fresh herbs and serve the soup ladled into warmed serving bowls with fresh crusty bread to dip in the beautiful fresh aromatic soup.

TANDOORI SPICED SALMON
Serves 4

A simple dish to prepare, soft, moist pieces of salmon, mildly spiced with ginger and garlic. This dish can easily be prepared before hand and left in the marinade until you are ready to serve, just bake in the oven for 10 minutes and serve, its simply delicious and very healthy.

Ingredients
4 x 175g/6oz salmon fillet portions or steaks
6 tbsps natural yoghurt
1 tsp garam masala
1 tsp paprika
small piece fresh ginger, peeled and grated
1/2 tsp ground cumin
2 garlic cloves, peeled and crushed
lime wedges to serve

1. Place the marinade ingredients together in a large bowl, season well with salt and freshly ground black pepper and mix thoroughly until all the ingredients are well combined.

2. Place the salmon pieces in the marinade and ensure they are coated completely in the spiced marinade, turning occasionally. Cover the bowl, then set aside in the fridge until you are ready to serve.

3. Preheat the oven to 200c/400f/Gas mark 6. Remove the salmon from the marinade and place onto a lightly greased baking tray, place in the preheated oven and cook for about

about 10 minutes or until the fish is just cooked through. Remove from the oven and serve immediately with lime wedges to spritz over the top and a dill sauce.

DILL SAUCE

Ingredients
4 tbsps Dijon mustard
2 tbsps caster sugar
2 egg yolks
4 tbsps white wine vinegar
400 ml olive oil
6 tbsps dill, finely chopped
sea salt and white pepper

1. Place the egg yolk, Dijon mustard, caster sugar, egg yolks and vinegar in a food processor or mixing bowl and blend or mix them together until well combined.

2. Slowly pour in the olive oil while blending or mixing until you have a thick mayonnaise consistency. Mix in the dill and salt and pepper to taste and serve at once.

Foreland Point & Lynmouth Bay

Paignton & Dartmouth Steam Railway

Totnes Castle

FISHERMANS PIE
Serves 6

Hearty, warming, indulgent and comforting.

Ingredients
300g/11oz smoked haddock fillet, pin bones removed
300g/11oz haddock fillet, pin bones removed
300g/11oz salmon fillet, pin bones removed
6 scallops, each cut in half, to make 2 thinner discs
110g/4oz large cooked peeled prawns
1 onion, peeled, sliced
750ml/1 1/4 pints milk
75ml/3fl oz white wine
110g/4oz frozen peas
3 hard boiled eggs, cut into quarters
3 tbsps freshly chopped parsley
50g/2oz plain flour
50g/2oz butter
salt and pepper

For the topping
1kg/2.2lb potatoes, peeled, cut into equal sized pieces
110g/4oz butter
75g/3oz grated cheddar cheese
splash of cream

1. Preheat the oven to 200c/400f/Gas mark 6. Place the milk and onions in a large shallow saucepan and bring up to the boil, then reduce the heat to a very gentle simmer.

FISHERMANS PIE/continued

2. Add the smoked haddock, haddock and salmon and cook very gently for 4-5 minutes. Remove the fish carefully with a slotted spoon and set aside to cool. Reserve the cooking milk for the sauce.

3. Melt the butter in a saucepan, add the flour and stir well to make a roux, gradually stir in warm milk, stirring constantly to create a smooth sauce, stir in the wine and simmer for 2-3 minutes. Season to taste with salt and freshly ground black pepper. Then set aside and keep warm.

4. When the fish is cool enough to handle, remove the skin and flake the fillet into large bite sized pieces. Place the fish into a suitably sized oven proof dish.

5. Meanwhile cook the potatoes in boiling salted water until tender, drain well, then mash until smooth, then beat in the butter and a splash of cream, season to taste with salt and black pepper.

6. Place the raw scallops, prawns, peas, parsley and eggs into the dish and combine with the flaked fish, ensuring all the fish and eggs are evenly distributed in the dish. Pour the sauce over the fish and carefully mix together ensuring all the fish is evenly coated in the sauce.

7. Carefully spoon the mashed potatoes over the filling to cover it completely, sprinkle over the grated cheese and place in the preheated oven for 25-30 minutes or until the topping is beautifully golden brown and the filling is bubbling hot.

DARTMOUTH PIE
Serves 6

This traditional pie, historically (and still locally) made with mutton, is full of medieval flavours. Pork provide a delicious, more readily available alternative.

Ingredients
1 1/2lb pork, thinly sliced
2 large onions, peeled and sliced
4 medium size cooking apples, peeled and sliced
2 tbsps of brown sugar
pinch of nutmeg
pinch of ground cinnamon
1/2 pint cider
8oz shortcrust pastry (prebought or preprepared)

1. Preheat the oven to 200c/400f/Gas mark 6. Mix together the brown sugar, nutmeg and cinnamon to make a sugar/spice mix.

2. In a deep oven-proof dish, place a layer of about half of the sliced pork then cover with a layer of half of the apples, half of the sugar/spice mix and a layer of half onions. Add a further layer of the remaining pork slices, apple slices, sugar/spice mix and onions slices then pour over the cider.

3. Roll out the pastry and cover the dish, making two holes for the steam to escape. Bake for 20 minutes then reduce the oven to 150c/300f/Gas mark 2 for a further 60 minutes with the pastry covered in foil to prevent burning. Serve with creamy mash.

EXETER STEW AND HERBY DOUGHBOYS
Serves 4-6

A traditional hearty stew from Exeter, served with plump herby dumplings affectionately called Doughboys In Devon.

Ingredients
900g/2lb braising steak cut in large chunks
2 tbsps plain flour
4 tbsps beef dripping
2 large onions, peeled, roughly chopped
3 large carrots, peeled, roughly chopped
1/2 swede, peeled, cut into chunks
40fl oz/2 pints beef stock
1 tsp vinegar

For the doughboys
175g/6oz plain flour
75g/3oz shredded beef suet
1 tsp baking powder
1 tsp salt
pinch of pepper
1 tsp dried mixed herbs
2 tbsps chopped fresh parsley

1. Toss the beef in half the flour seasoned with salt and freshly ground black pepper. In a large heavy based casserole dish, heat the beef dripping and fry the beef in batches until golden brown all over. Remove the meat and set aside. Preheat the oven to 180c/350f/Gas mark 4.

2. Add the onions, carrots and swede to the pan and cook for 3-4 minutes until the onions begin to soften. Sprinkle in the remaining flour and stir, cooking for a further minute.

3. Gradually add the hot beef stock and vinegar. Season to taste with salt and freshly ground black pepper. Return the beef to the casserole, cover with a lid and cook in the oven for 1 1/2 - 2 hours, stirring occasionally.

4. Meanwhile to make the doughboys, combine the flour, baking powder, salt, herbs and suet until mixed thoroughly. Add sufficient cold water to form a soft dough. Shape the dough into 8-10 small balls.

5. Remove the stew from the oven about half an hour before it is cooked and place the doughboys on top of the stew.

6. Return the stew to the oven and continue cooking until the meat is meltingly tender and the doughboys are well risen.

THYME ROASTED PORK LOIN WITH DEVON CIDER CREAM SAUCE

Serves 6

Delicious tender Pork with crispy crackling served with a rich cream sauce flavoured with local Devon cider.

Ingredients
1.5kg/3lb/5oz rolled boneless pork loin, skin scored
small bunch fresh thyme
150ml dry cider
100ml double cream

1. Preheat the oven to 200c/400f/Gas mark 6. Rub the pork skin with a little olive oil then season with coarse sea salt and the thyme leaves. Place the pork in a roasting tray and roast in the preheated oven for 1 1/2 hours basting occasionally.

2. Remove the pork from the oven, remove the crispy crackling and cover the pork loin with a sheet of tin foil and set aside to rest while you make the sauce.

3. Pour away any excess fat from the tray then place the tray over a medium heat on the stove. Add the cider to the pan and using a wooden spoon, scrape the base of the pan releasing all the sticky caramelised bits on the bottom of the tray. Add the double cream to the pan and stir well to combine and heat through.To serve, slice the rested pork loin and arrange on a large warmed serving plate. Spoon over the cider cream sauce and serve with the crackling cut into bite sized pieces. Serve with creamy mashed potatoes and seasonal green vegetables.

DEVON LAVER CAKES
Serves 2 - 4

Laver is an edible seaweed, with a high mineral content, particularly iodine and iron. The high iodine content gives the seaweed a distinctive flavour similar to that of olives or oysters. Brown in colour but boils down to a dark green pulp when prepared. The seaweed is boiled for hours and minced, then used to make laverbread.

Ingredients
450g/1lb prepared laver
50g/2oz pinhead oatmeal
50g/2oz streaky bacon

1. Combine the prepared laver with sufficient oatmeal to bring the mixture together until combined. In a large heavy based frying pan fry the streaky bacon rashers in a little oil and add spoonfuls of the laver and fry in the bacon fat for 4-5 minutes. Remove from the pan and serve with the crispy bacon rashers.

DEVONSHIRE CREAM TEA
Serves 8

Delicious warm scones, home made strawberry jam and fresh clotted Devon cream served with a refreshing pot of tea, the perfect British afternoon tea-time treat. The method of assembling a Devon cream tea, differs slightly from their neighbours next door in Cornwall. The Devon method is to split the scones in two, each half covered with clotted cream finished with a spoonful of strawberry jam.

In Cornwall the scone is first spread with strawberry jam, with the cream added as the topping.

For the scones
225g/8oz self raising flour
pinch of salt
1 tsp baking powder
50g/2oz butter
25g/1oz caster sugar
150ml milk/1/4 pint milk
1 egg, beaten for glazing

1. Preheat the oven to 220c/425f/Gas 7. Sift together the flour, salt and baking powder into a large bowl. Stir in the sugar, add the butter and using your fingertips rub into the flour to create a fine breadcrumb consistency. Add the milk a little at a time to form a smooth dough

2. Roll out the dough on a lightly floured surface to a thickness of 2cm/3/4 inches. Using a 5cm/2inch cutter, cut out the dough, using one sharp downward cut, do not twist the cutter as this will result in an uneven rise during baking.

3. Brush the top the scones with the beaten egg, ensuring no egg wash drips down the side of the scone as this will hinder the rising. Leave the scones to rest for 15 minutes. Bake in the preheated oven for 10-12 minutes until golden brown.

4. Remove from the oven, allow to cool slightly and serve while still warm. Serve the scones spread generously with clotted cream and topped with strawberry jam, simply delicious.

STRAWBERRY JAM

Yields approx 3kg/6.6lb

Ingredients
2kg/4.4lb strawberries
juice of 3 lemons
2kg/4.4lb jam sugar
small knob of butter

1. Place the whole strawberries in a large non metallic bowl, add the sugar and lemon juice, gently stir together, then cover with a tea towel and leave to stand overnight.

2. Place a saucer in the freezer, this will be used to teat the jam has set to the correct consistency later. Tip the fruit and juice into a large preserving pan or a 4.5 litre/8 pint heavy based saucepan. Heat gently, stirring to dissolve the sugar, do not boil until the sugar has dissolved.

3. Turn up the heat and boil hard for 4 minutes, take off the heat and test for setting point. Spoon a little jam onto the cold saucer.

4. After a couple of minutes gently push your finger through the cold jam, if it wrinkles up the jam is ready, if not re boil for a further 2 minutes or until setting point is reached.

5. Take off the heat and swirl in the butter, if the scum doesn't dissolve skim with a slotted spoon. Leave to cool for 10 minutes. Stir gently to distribute the fruit then pour into warmed sterilised jars, top with a cellophane disc and seal with a tight fitting lid. Store in a cool dark place.

WHITEPOT (RICE PUDDING)
Serves 8-10

Whitepot is a late Tudor, early Stuart recipe dating back to 1615 particularly associated with Devon and the South West of England. This baked rice pudding dish flavoured with rose water and cinnamon is traditionally finished with a topping of caramelised almonds called Comfits.

Ingredients
1 litre single cream
6 egg yolks
2 egg whites
110g/4oz caster sugar
1/2 tsp rose water
110g/4oz short grain pudding rice
110g/4oz currants
pinch of salt
1 tsp ground cinnamon

For the topping
50g/2oz blanched whole almonds
2 tsps sugar
1tsp water

1. Simmer the cream in a heavy based pan for 3-4 minutes over a low heat, whisking occasionally to prevent the cream burning. Stir in the rose water and the ground cinnamon and simmer for a further 2 minutes. Stir in the rice, remove from the heat and set aside to cool for 20 minutes. Preheat the oven to 180c/350f/Gas mark 4.

2. In a large mixing bowl, whisk together the egg yolks and whites then beat in the sugar until rich and creamy. When the cream has cooled whisk it into the egg and sugar mixture and stir in the currants.

3. Pour the mixture into an ovenproof dish and bake for an hour, after 20 minutes remove from the oven and give the mixture a really good stir and return to the oven Stir again in a further 20 minutes, adding a little more milk or cream if the mixture is getting too thick.

4. Sprinkle a little extra sugar over the top and continue cooking for the last 20 minutes to develop a golden crust on top.

5. Meanwhile to make the topping, lightly toast the almonds in a dry frying pan over a medium heat. When the almonds are lightly toasted, add the sugar and cook for a minute or two until the sugar has melted then add the water to make a simple sugar syrup.

6. Coat the almonds in the sugar syrup, then remove to a bowl to cool. The almonds will stick together as they cool, but can easily be broken apart.

7. Remove the pudding from the oven and sprinkle over the sugared almonds. The pudding can be eaten hot or cold. Serve the pudding spooned into bowls with a little extra cream if desired.

NEWTON ABBOT CIDER CAKE

The perfect tea time treat with a fruity little kick.

Ingredients
8 tbsps cider
275g/10oz dried mixed fruit, (sultanas, currants & raisins)
175g/6oz butter100ml
175g/6oz light brown sugar
3 eggs, beaten
225g/8oz self raising flour
2 tsps mixed spice

1. Soak the dried fruit in the cider for at least a couple of hours but it's best to leave overnight if you have the time. Preheat the oven to 180/350f/Gas mark 4.

2. Cream together the butter and sugar until pale, light and fluffy, gradually add the eggs one at a time, beating thoroughly between each addition. Sieve the flour and mixed spice into the creamed egg and butter mixture.

3. Stir in the soaked dried fruit and stir well until thoroughly combined. Spoon the cake mixture into a greased and lined 22cm x 7cm deep loose bottomed cake tin.

4. Bake in the oven for 50-60 minutes or until well risen and golden brown and a skewer inserted into the centre comes out clean. Remove from the oven, leave to cool slightly in the tin, then remove from the tin and allow to cool on a wire cooling rack. When cool, cut into slices and serve with clotted cream.

RASPBERRY RIPPLE AND CLOTTED CREAM ICE

Serves 4

Ingredients
2 large free range eggs
150g/5oz caster sugar
275ml/1/2 pint double cream
250g/9oz clotted cream
275ml/1/2 pint full fat milk
250g/9oz fresh raspberries
1 tbsp icing sugar

1. Whisk the egg in a large bowl until light and fluffy, then gradually add the caster sugar and continue whisking.

2. Pour in the double cream, clotted cream and milk into the egg mixture and mix well. Spoon the mixture into an ice cream machine and churn until almost frozen. If making by hand, spoon the ice cream into a 2 litre plastic freezer container and freeze for 3 hours, then beat with a whisk until smooth and return to the freezer for a further 3 hours. Repeat this process 2-3 times, then freeze for 2 hours.

3. Meanwhile, lightly crush the raspberries with the icing sugar with the back of a fork. When the ice cream has frozen to the soft scoop stage, gently fold in the crushed raspberries to create a ripple effect. Return to the freezer until solid. Remove the ice cream from the freezer 20 minutes before serving and spoon into bowls, simply delicious.

DEVONSHIRE SPLITS
Makes 10

Affectionately called Chudleighs or Devon Buns, Devonshire Splits are raised yeast buns served for afternoon tea traditionally served filled with clotted cream and jam.

Ingredients
450g/1lb plain flour
pinch of salt
1 x 7g sachet dried yeast
25g/1oz caster sugar
50g/2oz butter, melted
284ml/1/2 pint tepid milk
milk to glaze

To serve
clotted cream, or lightly whipped double cream
raspberry jam
icing sugar to dust

1. Sift the flour and salt into a large bowl, stir in the dried yeast and caster sugar. Stir together the melted butter and tepid milk, then add to the flour and mix well to create a smooth soft dough.

2. Turn the dough onto a lightly floured board and knead for 5-10 minutes until soft and smooth. Place the dough in a clean bowl, cover with a clean towel and leave to prove in a warm place for an hour or until the dough has doubled in size. Meanwhile preheat the oven to 200c/400f/Gas mark 6.

3. Turn out the proved dough onto a lightly floured surface and divide into 10 pieces. Knead each piece lightly for a minute or two and shape into rounds. Place the balls onto a lightly greased baking sheet. spaced well apart. Cover lightly with cling film and leave to prove once again in a warm place until doubled in size.

4. Brush the top of the buns lightly with milk, then bake in the preheated oven for12-15 minutes until well risen and golden brown. Remove from the oven and leave to cool on a wire rack.

5. Using a sharp knife, cut the buns open on a slight angles and fill generously with clotted cream and jam and finish with a dusting of icing sugar.

DEVONSHIRE JUNKET
Serves 4

A subtle flavoured dish also known as Damask Cream.

Ingredients
570ml/1 pint fresh single cream
3 tbsps caster sugar
2 tsps rennet essence
large pinch of freshly grated nutmeg
1 tbsp brandy
4 tbsps clotted cream or double cream
1 tsp rose water
rose petals to decorate

1. Place the single cream and 2 tablespoons of the sugar in a saucepan. Heat gently until tepid (36.9c/98.4f) stirring

until the sugar has dissolved. Stir in the rennet, nutmeg and brandy then pour into a serving dish. Leave to stand for 2-3 hours until set.

2. When the junket is set, mix the remaining sugar, cream and rose water together and spoon carefully over the top. Finish the dish with a sprinkling of rose petals.

DEVONSHIRE CLOTTED CREAM FUDGE
Makes 36 small pieces

The ultimate sweet decadence!

Ingredients
275g/11oz caster sugar
110g/4oz golden syrup
225g/8oz clotted cream
1/2 tsp vanilla extract
butter for greasing

1. Grease a 20cm/8inch square tin lightly with butter. Place all the ingredients in a large heavy based saucepan and heat very gently, stirring continuously until the sugar has completely dissolved.

2. Bring to the boil covered with a lid for 3 minutes. Remove the lid and continue cooking until the mixture reaches 115 degrees centigrade on a sugar thermometer.

3. Remove the fudge from the heat and allow to cool slightly, then beat the mixture until the mixture turns thick and creamy. Transfer the fudge into the prepared greased tray and leave to cool for 30 minutes.

4. Mark the fudge with the tip of a knife to form small squares.

5. Leave to cool completely before cutting into pieces and tucking in.

BARNSTAPLE FAIR PEARS
Serves 4

The rich and abundant pear orchards of Devon were used to supply stalls at the Barnstaple Fair. Originally the pears would have been simmered in the local cider or scrumpy. This recipe uses red wine but can quite easily be substituted for cider.

Ingredients
4 large ripe comice pears
25g/1oz blanched almonds, slit in half
50g/2oz caster sugar
300ml/1/2 pint red wine
2 cloves

1. Peel the pears,leaving the stalk intact, then remove the core from the underside using an apple corer. Spike the pears with the split almonds.

2. Place the sugar, wine and the cloves in a saucepan big enough to hold the pears and heat gently until the sugar has dissolved.

3. Stand the pears up in the simmering wine, cover with a lid and cook gently for 20-25 minutes or until the pears are really tender but still holding their shape. Baste the pears as they are cooking occasionally with the red wine.

4. Remove the pears with a slotted spoon and place them in a dish. Increase the heat and boil the wine until it has reduced by half and become syrupy. Pour the syrup over the pears and serve either hot or cold with clotted cream or natural yoghurt.

EXETER PUDDING
Serves 6

A traditional recipe from Exeter, of a layered sponge pudding.

Ingredients
150g/5oz fresh white breadcrumbs
50g/2oz ratafia/amaretti biscuits
75g/3oz caster sugar
75g/3oz butter
3 tbsps dark rum
450g/1lb blackcurrant or apricot jam
zest of 1 lemon
150ml/1/4 pint double cream
3 eggs
25g/1oz plain flour
6 trifle sponges

1. Preheat the oven to 180c/350f/Gas mark 4. Mix together 110g/4oz of the breadcrumbs with the flour and lemon zest, then rub in the butter. Lightly grease a 25cm/10inch pudding basin with butter and coat the base with the remaining breadcrumbs. Cover the base with the ratafia biscuits. Place a layer of the prepared breadcrumb mixture over the ratafia biscuits.

2. Spread the trifle sponges with the jam of your choice and place these in the dish as the next layer. Combine the eggs with the cream and mix thoroughly. Spread the remaining breadcrumb mixture over the sponges, then pour over the egg and cream mixture. Drizzle the rum over the top and bake in the preheated oven for 50 -60 minutes.